AF223637

The Unmistakable **Possibility** of Us

poems by

r.c. perez

Copyright © 2023 r.c. perez

All rights reserved. This book or any portion thereof may not be reproduced or used in any manner whatsoever without the express written permission of the publisher except for the use of brief quotations in a book review and certain other noncommercial uses permitted by copyright law.

ISBN: 978-1-7776334-3-1 (Print)
ISBN: 978-1-7776334-4-8 (eBook)

Cover art by Ryan Dean Haas
◎ @ryandeanhaas
Book cover design by Caroline Bieri
www.carolinebieri.de

ignovionwrites @gmail.com
◎ @ignovionwrites

introduction

How do you forgive yourself for not becoming the person you wanted to be?

Somewhere between now and the early days when we thought we could be anything, dreams died, and we never buried them. To this day they haunt us. And while it wasn't entirely our fault, we beat ourselves up over it. So how then, do we move forward from it?

This book is about the humbling process of slowly accepting what life has dealt us and making the most out of it—that while we mourn for our past, we look forward to the amazing possibility of who we still can be. It is not about What Never Was, but What Can Be. It is not an apology, but a promise.

Chapter I (of trusting the process). This chapter explores themes of depression, longing, failure, and regret. It gives you the space to acknowledge, feel, and process your pain while at the same time ignites hope that in your sadness, something good will come out.

Chapter II (of embracing change). This chapter invites you to think of all the possibilities that lie ahead once you take a leap of faith. The poems will encourage you to keep working on yourself while getting excited about what the future can bring.

Chapter III (of searching for life's meaning). "What am I here for?" This chapter is about rediscovery, redirection, recalibration. It's about finding a sense of purpose and the realization that it's never too late to dream again. You have time to make it come true.

Chapter IV (of growing in love). "And what else brings more promise than the arrival of love?" This final chapter explores the idea of love as a process of growing and knowing oneself. It is an attempt to present love in a less idealized way while keeping the same optimistic feeling that comes with loving someone.

Taken together, these chapters will take you on a journey through familiar feelings of worthlessness and stagnation and the rediscovery of oneself to find the motivation to live, to love, and to dream again.

Ultimately, this collection is an ode to the indomitable human spirit, a tribute to our undying dreams, and a celebration of the resilience we all possess to still make things happen.

If you ever once dreamed, if you ever once failed, this book is for you.

table of contents

Also by r.c. perez
Magic of the Modest

"This – / The spreading wide my narrow Hands /
To gather Paradise –"
—— **Emily Dickinson**

for the people
we are yet to become

I.

UNKNOWN

Strangers
to ourselves
we've become.
We ache, we mourn
for who we were
once.

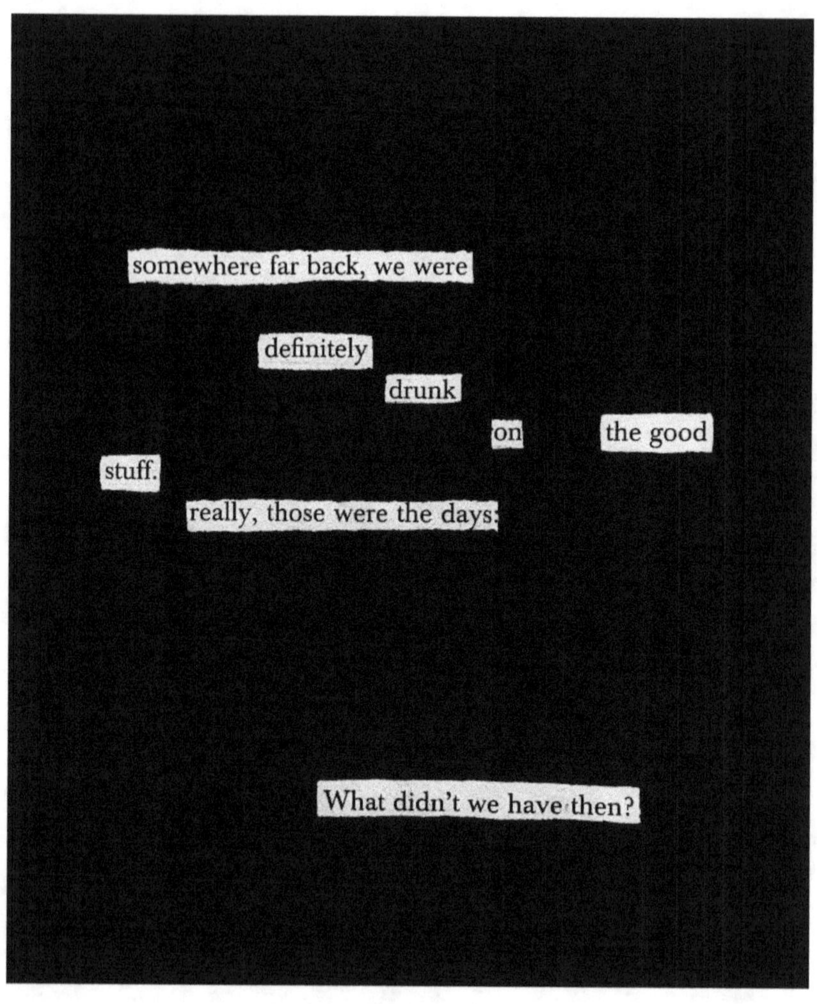

GOOD OLD DAYS

DARKER

When I say
it is dark in here,
I mean loneliness
casts itself
upon all of me;

I mean it is the shadow
of all the things
I cannot be;

I mean pull me
out of here.

STAY

Tell me it won't always
be this way.

Tell me it will only
get better from here.

That on your side,
there are still
beautiful things.

That sometimes when all
falls silent, I cross your mind—

and you remember
all our good times.
And it makes you smile.

I will know then
that I'm still here.

I promise, I will stay.

Pain,

if you are
a thing that flows,
let it be melted gold.

Out of broken pieces,
let it create
something
          beautiful.

PARALLELS

I carry this weight
inside of me
—all the grief and regret,
so real but no clear
origin—
and it makes me wonder:
in the multitude
of universes
where I exist,

am I repeating
the same mistakes over
and over again?

Perhaps this
is sadness
— to never be
needed.

DEAD DREAMS

Long are they gone
but we won't let go.
We burn the night
thinking about
what never was.

And sometimes
when sorrow seeps
we stay up,
dancing with the ghosts
of all the people
we didn't become.

EACH DAY A MOURNING

Don't we all die
a little death
each day,

as we wake up
farther and farther away
from the days
we still believed
we could be anything?

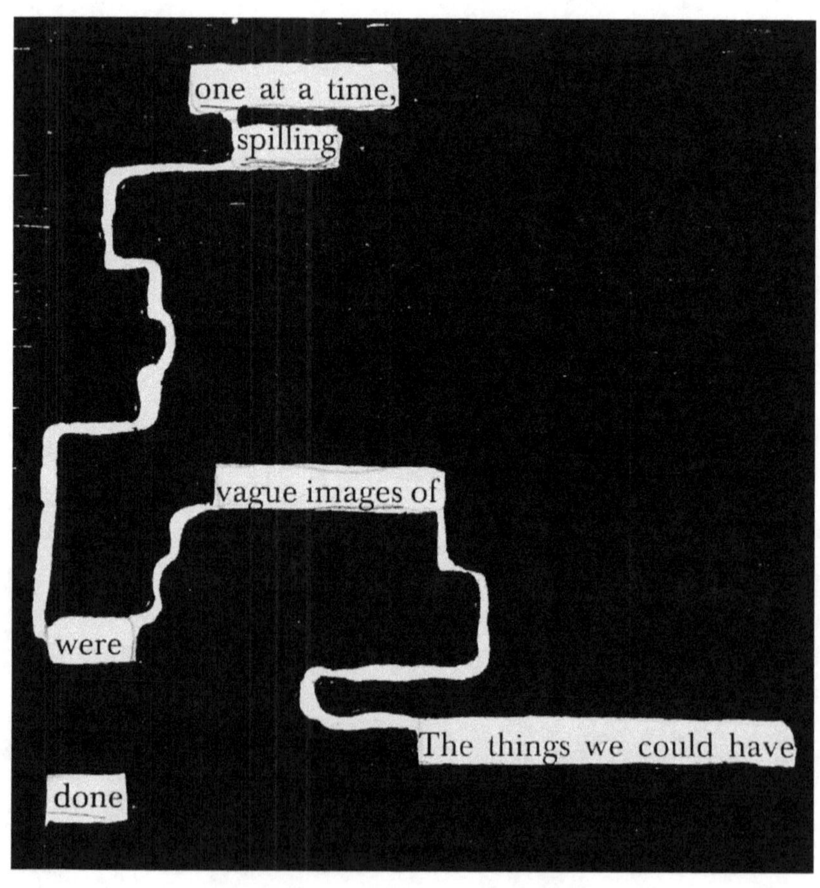

one at a time,
spilling
vague images of
were
The things we could have
done

RUSH

So loud, so fast, so busy
this world has come to be.

Always I am terrified
of getting left behind,
but God, I
am so tired.

Some days I pretend
that if I just wish hard enough,
that if I just stay still,
the world will stop spinning

—please, I can't keep up
any longer.

CITIES

When have we become
a city?

Full of life
and joy, it seems
—one which never sleeps
and always busy
but is not a home
to anybody.

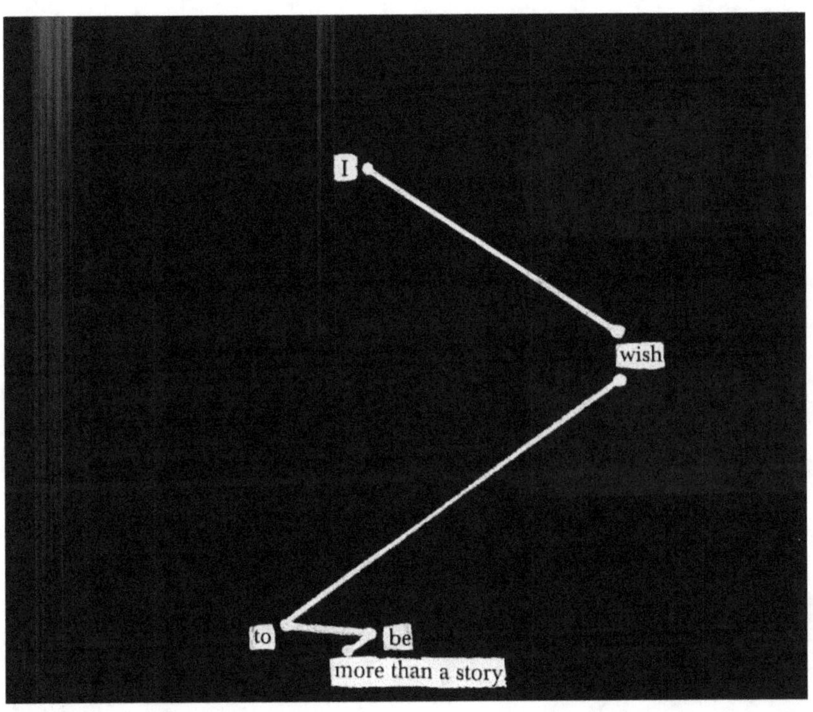
I
wish
to
be
more than a story

Today, the birds noticed
that your laughter
has not been quite the same.

The stars lamented
that your eyes
used to twinkle.

And the pavement could swear
there was music before
in your every step.

I guess everybody
has just been missing you

a lot, lately.

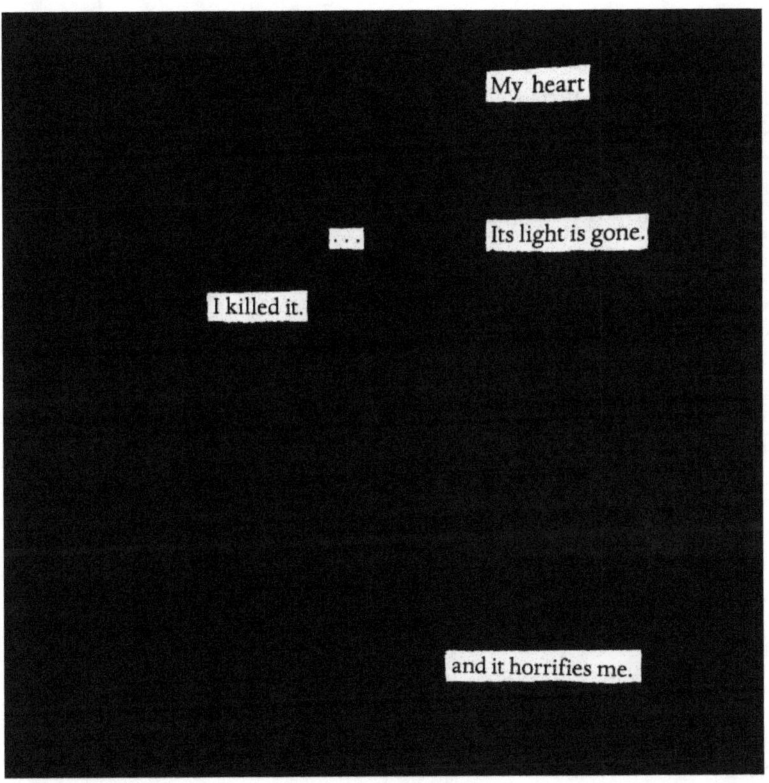
My heart
. . .
Its light is gone.
I killed it.
and it horrifies me.

ENOUGH

If all you ever did today
was to get up,
let it be enough.

If it felt like the world
asked for too much
and there was too little to give,
let it be enough.

Among the list of things undone,
add the word *survive*.
Tick the box.
Let it be enough.

TOMORROW

Old friend,
be patient.

Are you at the door
waiting?

Old friend,
I'm getting there.

Soon I'll be brave
to face the world again.

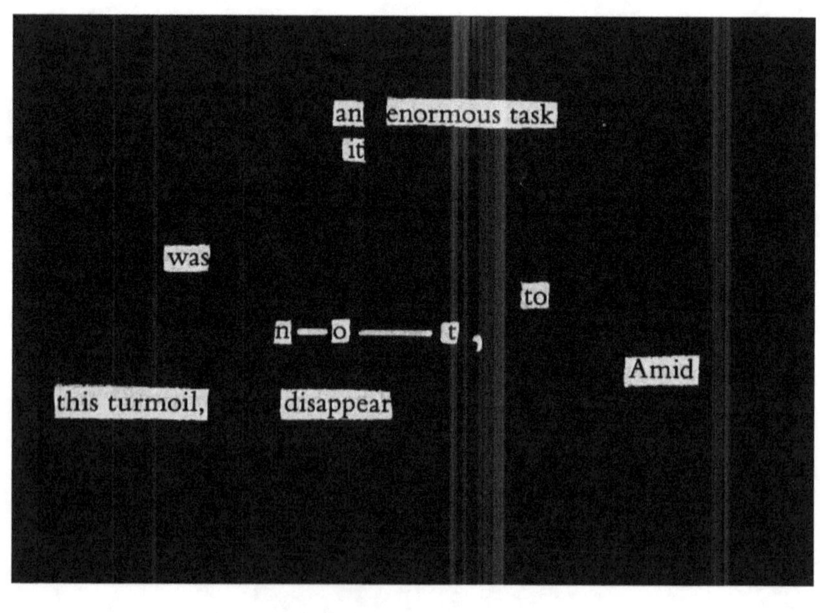
an enormous task
it

was
                              to
                                        Amid
this turmoil,   disappear
n — o — t ,

ON GRIEF

Still living.
Still real.
Still among us.

And more than we are
willing to admit,
we still ache
from an emptiness
we do not talk about.

what
bittersweet

memory.

we
wrap   around ourselves.

....

the past never leaves-

Most nights,
it seems most right
to imagine anything
other than what was.

FEAST

This
is what we crave
—the vague, the maybe.

Uncertainty
feeds fantasy,
and boy
do I prepare
the most
sumptuous feast.

We
weren't in love.
We were just dreamers Caught in the dream of
what might have been.

INSTEAD

Perhaps,
it was too little
too late. We—
already too broken,
too hurt.

Let's meet instead
after this one,
in different bodies,
wearing scars
from all the wounds
that didn't heal
in this lifetime.

THE ORIGIN OF LONELINESS

In some place
or other—
somewhere I didn't go
—someone I would have loved
is longing silently
for the person
I didn't
choose to be.

He won't be coming;
please,
forgive me.

LIKE LIGHTNING

Swiftly,
love came
like lightning
to us.

Swiftly, too,
it left.

And I wonder,
does love ever strike
the same two people
twice?

LIMITED
VOCABULARY

Sometimes,
the words
I miss you
escape me.

So instead,
I say
I build a body
out of memory
in places where
you used to be.

WARS

Every storm, I have learned,
is an invitation to be strong.
Because if I close my eyes
on a cold, stormy night
as rain drops on the roof
like tiny little bombs,
winds hurl, thunder rumbles,
and lightning flashes on occasion
—if I whisper your name
or shout it out loud even—
no one is going to come running.
You won't hear me, no,
you will not be there
for the saving.

The night is too preoccupied
and I am not the only one at war.

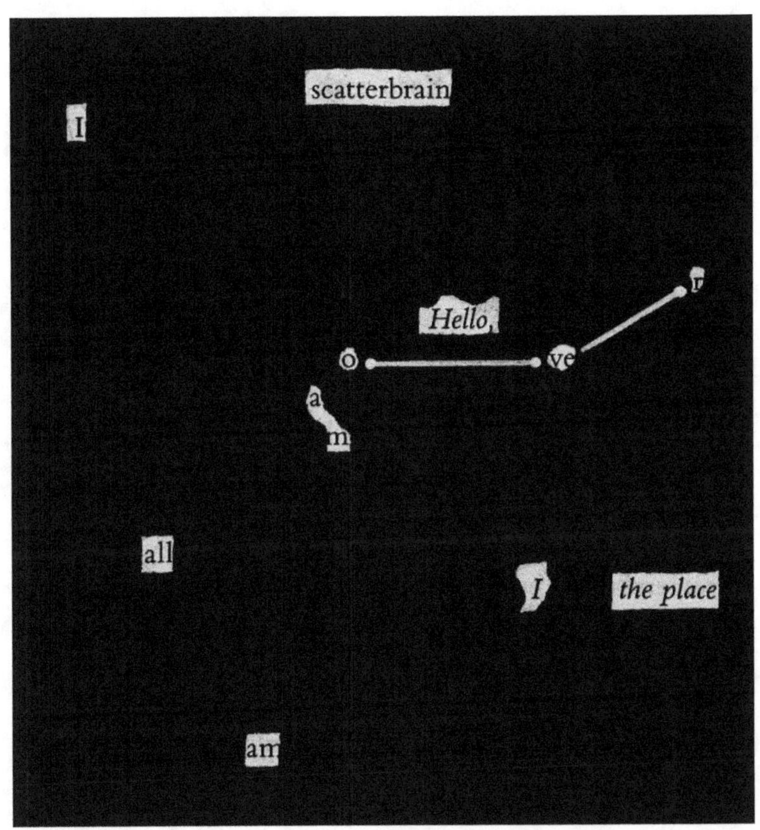

A MESS

YOU ARE ALIVE, AND DREAMING IS FAMILIAR

You know this all too well—
your morning coffee whose taste
you could only describe in sips
that spell

        h – o – p – e

You have seen this before—
this sky the colour of something
that once saw you dream.

They still come, though few and
far between: days like this, they come.

Listen to the breaking of dawn.
It is telling you

        you are not over yet.

THE PATIENCE OF BUTTERFLIES

Is there anything else
out there for me?
I asked in contempt,

and bless these butterflies
—how very quickly
they humbled me.

HOW TO WIN

Summon that silent strength
in you.

Call upon it
and wake it from slumber:

To smile at adversities
and emerge in wisdom.
To dust it off every time
you fall, and with
ever-growing humility,
to begin again.

You are strong,
though not the one-shot kind,
though not in the way
that charges headlong
and gets it the first time.

Your fight is in the way
you sit, bloody and bruised,
and take it in—
for the next times,
for the second tries.

Trust me, even now
you are winning.

Strength,

if you are
a thing that flows,
let it be water
that hollows out
a stone—

drop by drop,
calm, and
constant.

RENASCENCE

And I declare this
with all the faith in my heart:

that you will learn to live again—

loud as the scent of the earth
after the rain,

bold as sunshine feels
on your skin,

wild as the waves
splashing against your feet,

and tender as the taste
of all possibilities
in the flight of birds.

II.

REBIRTH

What lovely sight—
this vernal vindication:
that after the bludgeoning
comes the burgeoning.

To you, who kept faith,
arise! Everything around,
once again, is alive.

And so are you.

FLOW

of roads
that lead
to another;
of doorways
to another place;
of turning the page
as one chapter ends;
of river mouths, of new
moons, of springs, of daybreaks.
life keeps moving, and where
there is an end, there is beginning.
remember, you can always start again.

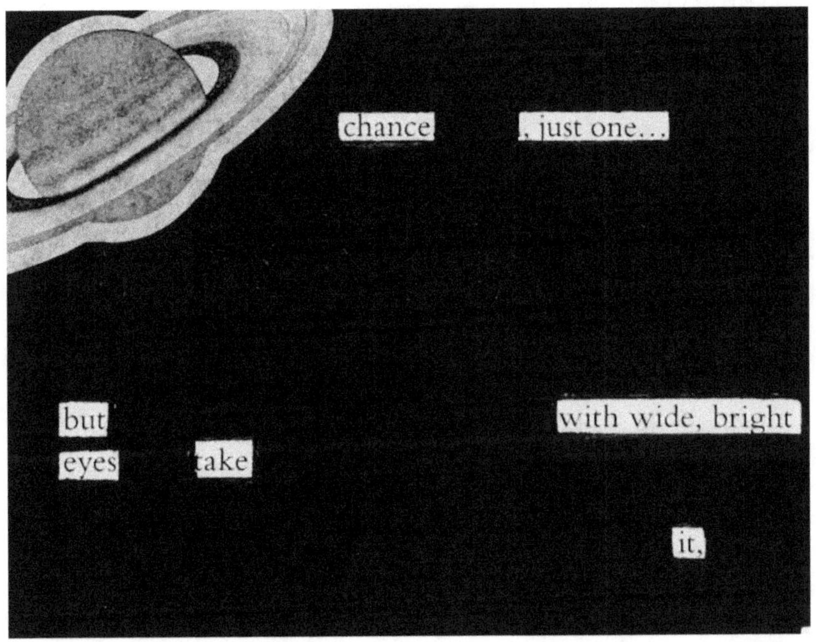
chance   , just one…

but   with wide, bright
eyes   take

                                              it,

BETTER HALF

This life—
spent half of it
at the edge
of comfort.

At last,
a leap of faith!

And if I should miss,
let me fall
among heroes
and monsters
in battlefields.

Give me one
glorious adventure.

If I should die,
let me die
living.

This
is growth:
this necessary ache—
yes, everything hurts now,
but I'm learning; I'm becoming.

WHAT ABOUT LIFE

What about the unknown,
what about the unfamiliar
that you fear?

What about being on your toes,
what about learning,
what about new friends and lovers,
what about being in awe of the other worlds
you wouldn't otherwise have seen?

What about living
that makes you cower?

Go out there.

It's all about
the happy little surprises.

Courage,

if you are
a thing that flows,
let it be cold sweat
on palms of
trembling hands.

Let it be something
    born of fear.

TRAVELLERS

And so it seems
you have been on this road
before.
Stations and tracks
in blur.

Tell me where
this story stops
and I will alight at once.
Show me where
to embark on a new one.

MANIFESTATION

I imagine a future
—happy, proud, fulfilled.
I want it to be anything
other than regret.

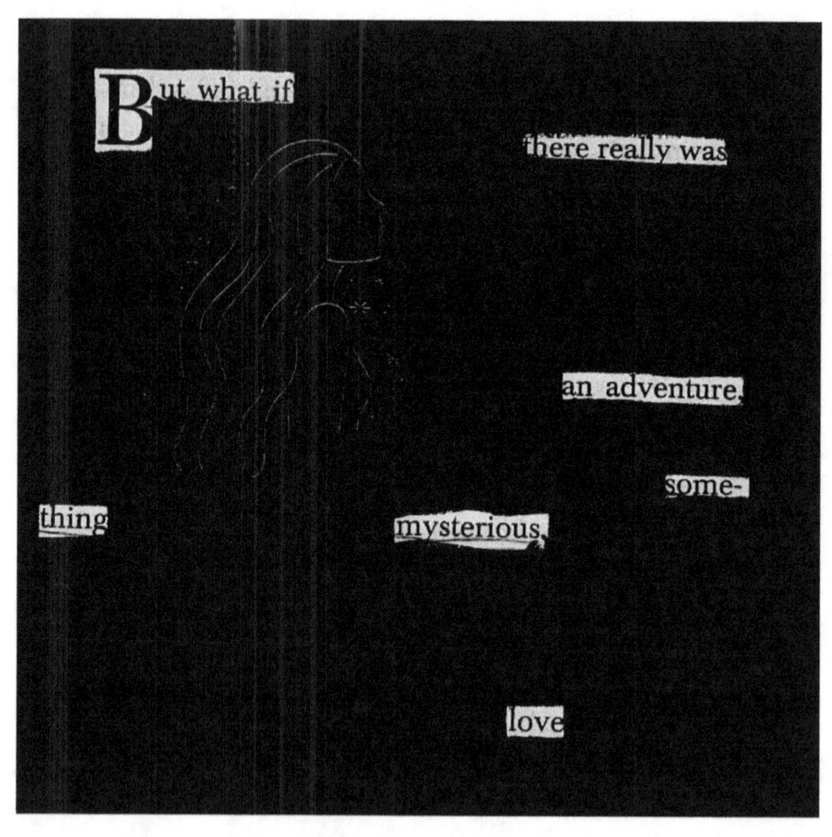

WHAT YOU'D MISS

CARRY ON

I'm going to leave
everything behind.
I will travel light
—no room for
excess, just
an empty suitcase
to be filled with love
I have yet to find.

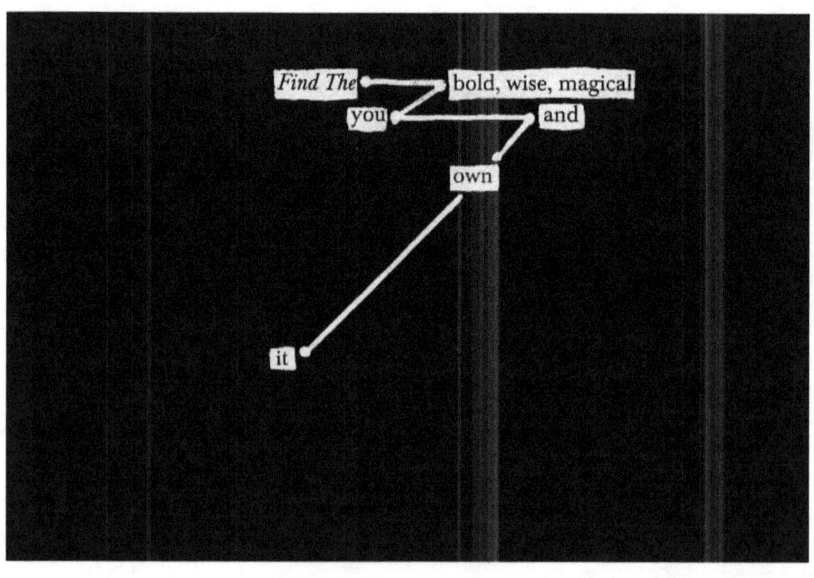

Find The
bold, wise, magical.
you
and
own
it

Go after
what warms
your heart.

Chase the light.
Feel alive

—bloom,
summer's child

What are flaws
if not excuses
for why you
can't be?

JBY

And be that as it may,
all things considered,
at the end of the day,
in spite of,
and regardless,
just be you.

BLINDSPOT

How easy it must be
to convince yourself
you are unworthy.

But if you could only
see, oh I swear,
if you could
only see.

AS YOU ARE

Here is a place of magic
where all beauty lies.
If you must come,
come as you are.

WHAT MUST BREAK

Silence, for what
needs to be said.

Glass ceilings, for what
cannot be contained.

The ground, for what shall
rise above it.

The dawn, for what comes
after the dark.

Stigmas and cycles and chains,
for what needs to end.

Yourself, for what shall
become of you after.

Sometimes, things break
so light can enter,

so something can grow,
so the old can usher in the new.

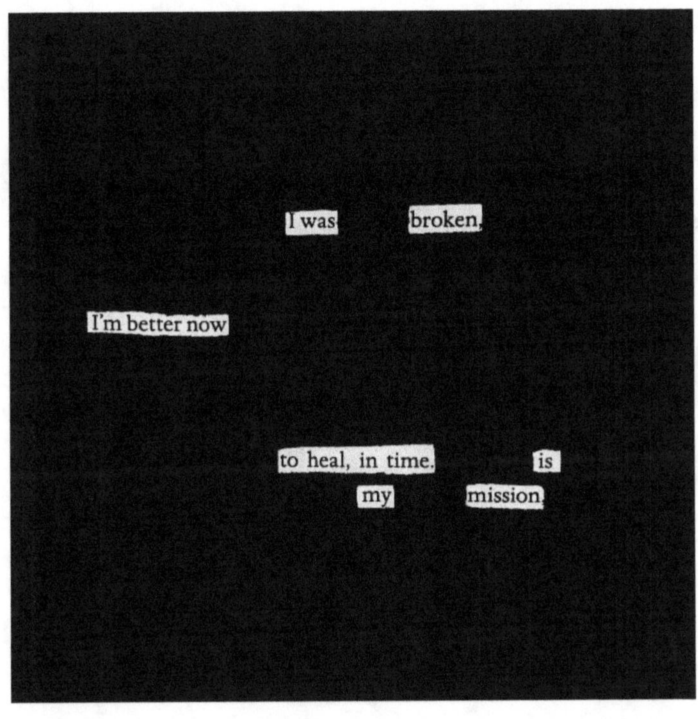
I was broken,
I'm better now
to heal, in time. is
my mission.

LATELY

Lately,
I have been hating
my reflection
less and less.

Lately,
I have been wishing
more and more
for myself.

And I have to believe:
this, too, is forgiveness.

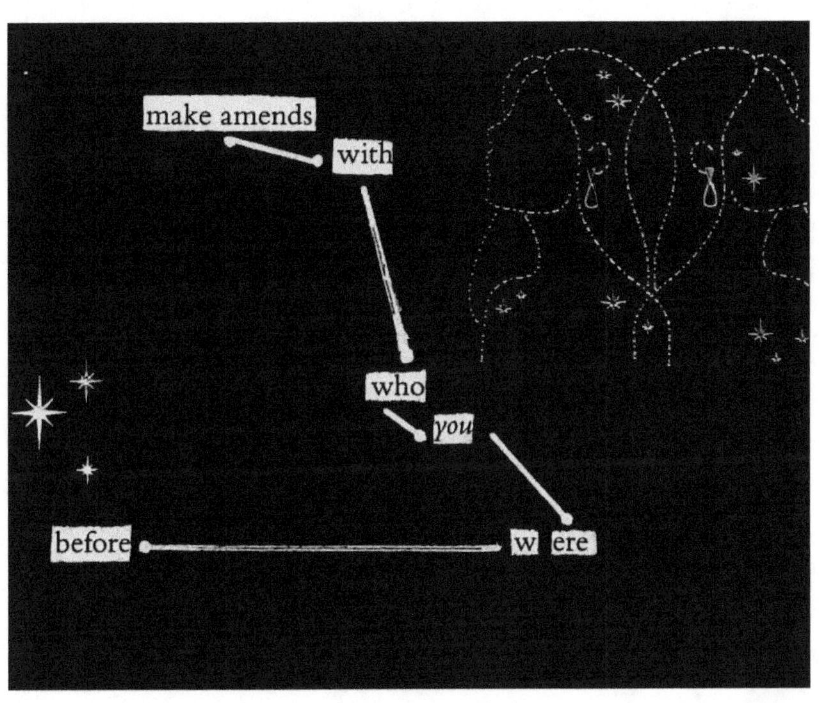

make amends
with
who
you
before
w ere

LIGHTHOUSE

And though the dark
seems so inviting,

that light in you
—never let it dim.

Somewhere out in the sea
love is trying to find
its way back to you.

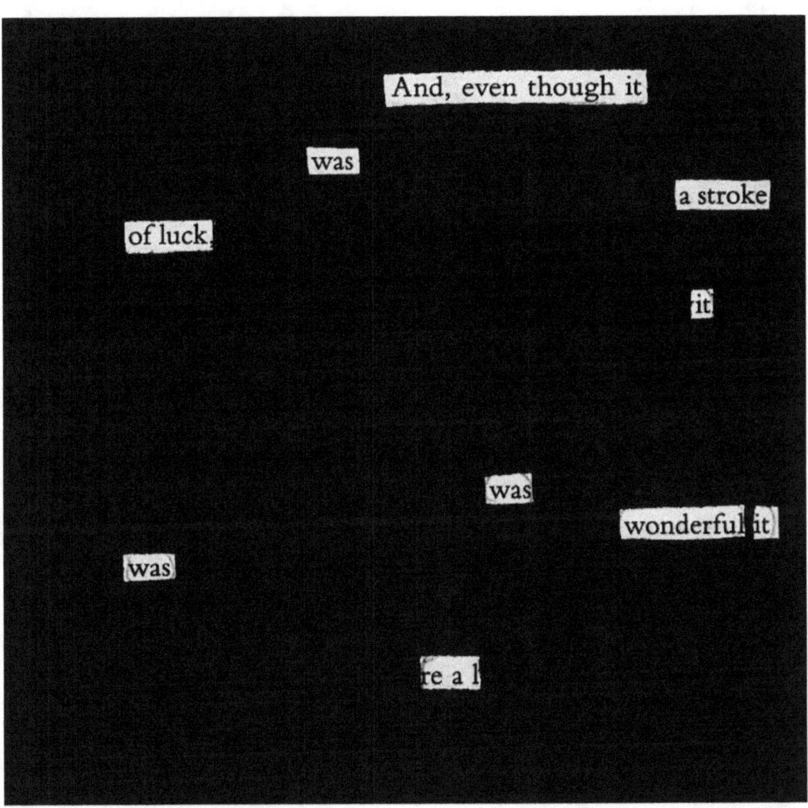

And, even though it
was
a stroke
of luck,
it
was
wonderful it
was
re a l

We love.
We lose.
We break.
But ultimately,
WE MEND.

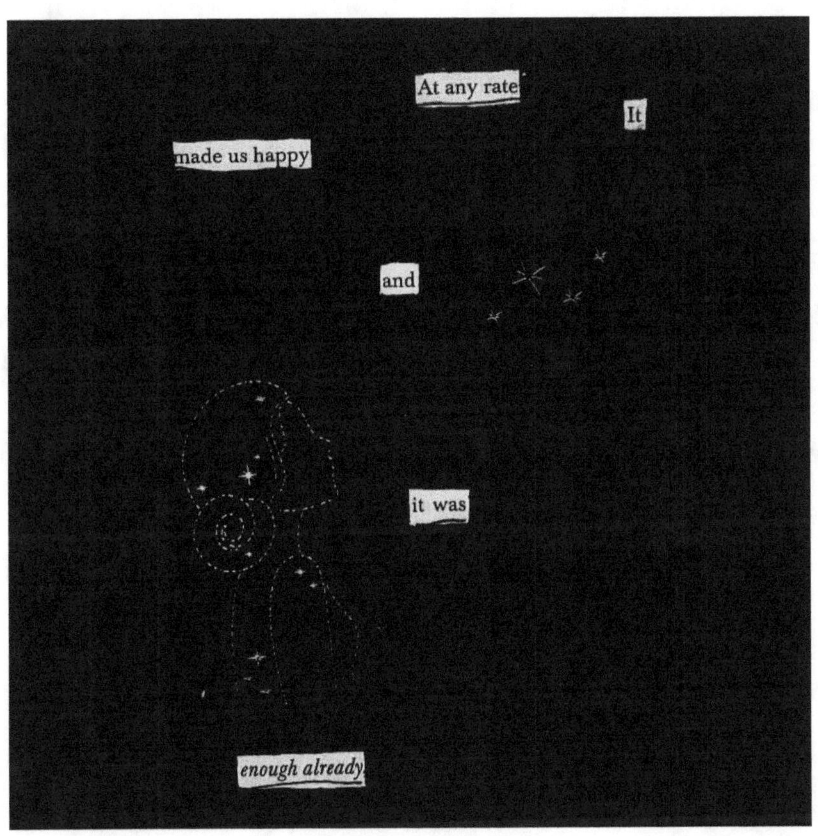

NO REGRETS

SOMETHING GOOD IS HAPPENING—

The bus is on time;
the coffee tastes
divine; sun's out,
and everyone
is smiling.

The air is
fresh and crisp,
and things
look promising.

I think
I am ready
to fall in love
again.

you   let the whole thing go

                    And yet,

isn't it funny

                    Isn't it strange
                    to find

more   for yourself?

RARITIES

Today was a treat—

I am licking my lips
for every bit
of it left.

Can I have
more,
please?

CONSPIRACY
THEORY

Talk to the wind,
scream to the sun,
tell the flowers
what your heart
desires.

Today is dazzling
with absurd harmony,
and I have never been
more sure—
this is the time
your stars align.

SMALL WINS

What am I
if I'm not seeking
for a glimpse of wisdom?

What am I
if I'm not hoping
for just a sliver of chance?

What am I
if I'm not striving
for an inch of progress,
however little it is?

I look back
and take the counsel
of my past;
I look ahead
and take a step
at a time.

TODAY'S ESSENTIAL QUESTIONS:

1. ~~Was I outstanding?~~
2. Was I kind?
3. Was I patient with myself?

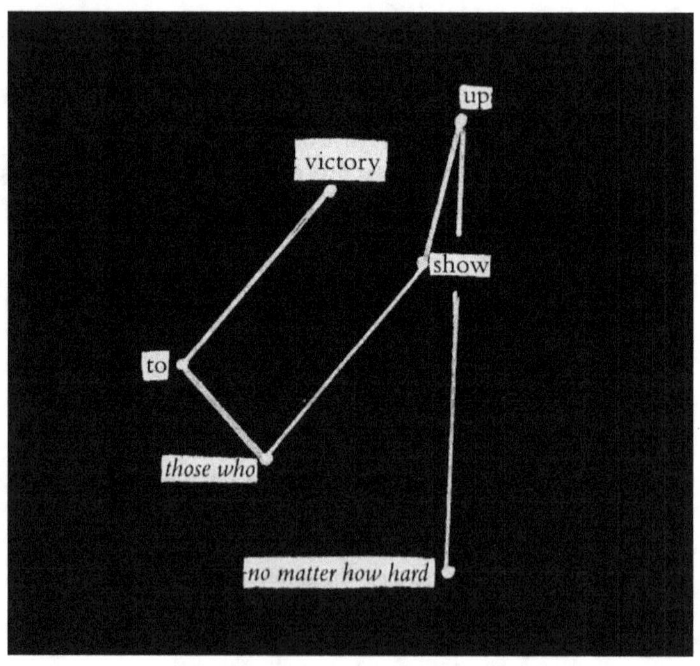

up
victory
show
to
those who
no matter how hard

ROAD TO SUCCESS

Try,
fall,
and try

because how else
will you make it?

There is no
other way.

GRIT

How many times
has the world
said *no* to you?

How many times,
those dreams, has
it tried to crush?

And how many times
did you refuse
to give up?

Every.
Single.
Time.

So here's to a stubborn soul.
Here's to a rebel.
Here's to a dreamer
who finds ways
and makes things happen.

And then it happened…
and
It felt as if
all
The light
dimmed to the
brightness
of
you.

THE MOON SHINES BRIGHTEST TONIGHT

It was almost as if
they could not believe
you could shine this much.

Night by night,
brighter and brighter,
and no one
even realized.

Yet here you are—
this, the culmination,
wholeness
on full display.

This is your night.

ODE ON THINGS THAT FLOW

To be melted gold
that seals broken
pieces together.

To be the rivers
that give birth
to civilizations.

To be the blood
in your veins
that keeps you alive.

Oh, to be a thing
that refuses to stay still!

THAT WHICH SUSTAINS

Is it not light
and warmth
we seek?

Is it not
what we spend
all our lives
chasing?

So it is light
and warmth
we will give.

When nowhere else,
we will turn
to each other.

FACADES

A billion faces,
a billion stories.
We are all more
than meets the eye.

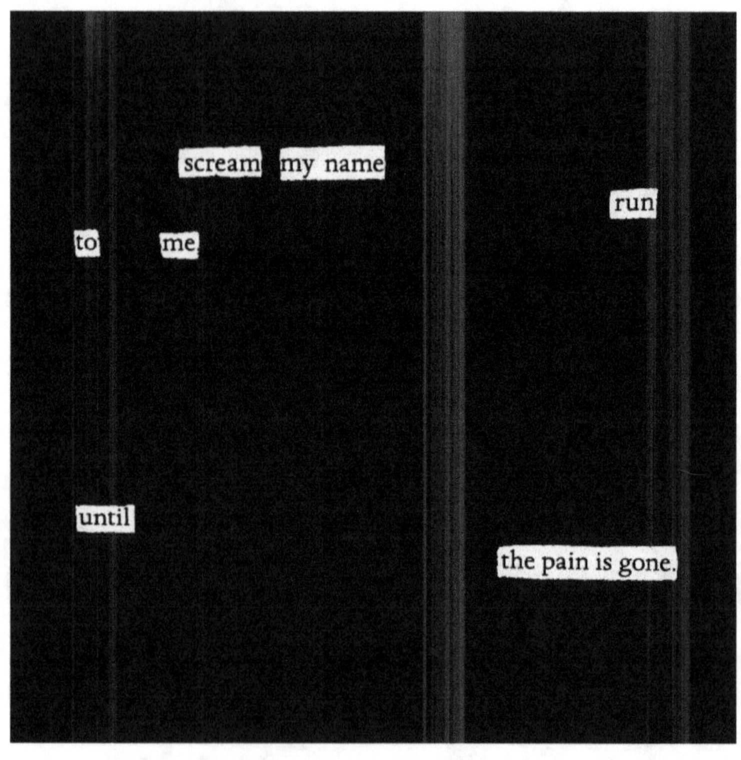

scream my name
run
to me
until
the pain is gone.

Love,

if you are
a thing that flows,
let it be the blood
in our veins.

Let it be
	necessary,
let it be
	in all of us.

HOW TO TEND A HEART

Not
of poison, nor
of blades.

These lips,
may they be made
of sunlight
and water.

That if in the heart
is a garden, may
the words I speak to others
bring forth their most
magnificent flowers.

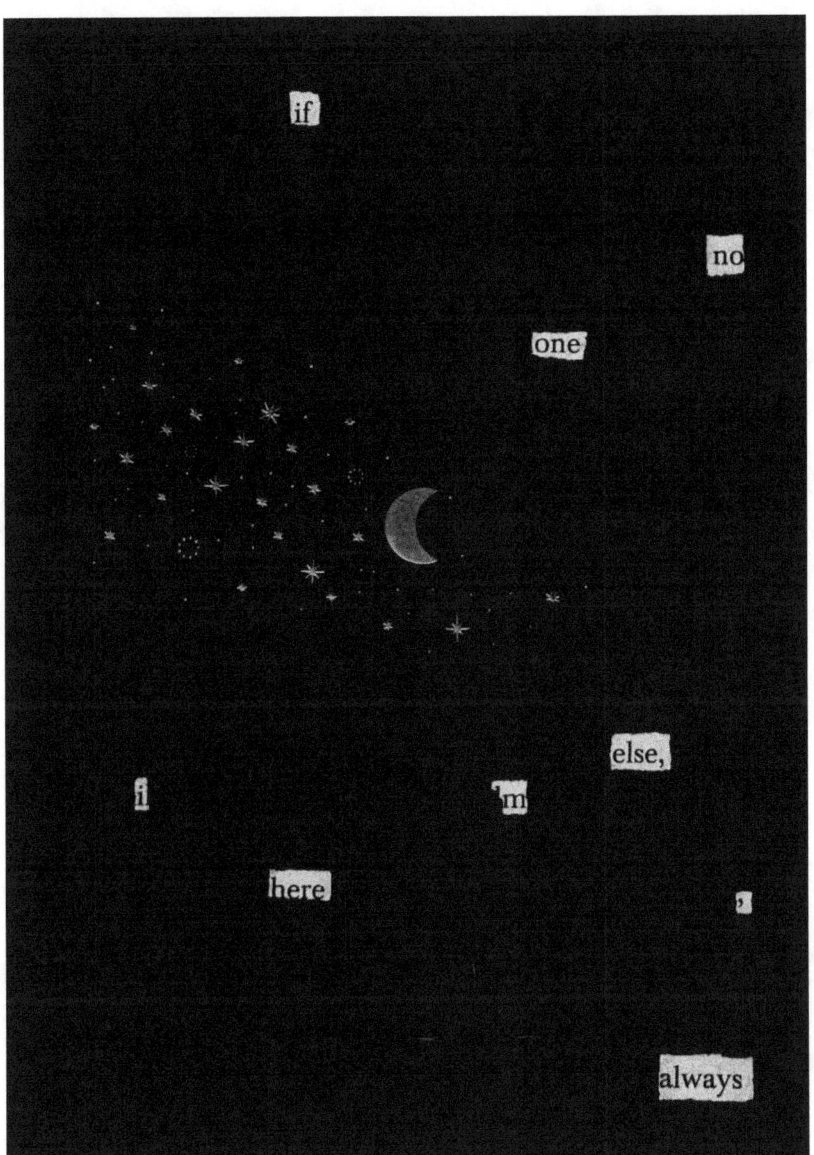
if
no
one
else,
i 'm
here
,
always

EMANCIPATION

Maybe this is what
an embrace is for—

that when all else fails,
while our arms cling
to the curves
of each other's backs
we could tell ourselves:

Someday, wings
will grow from there.

And I'll take you with me
when I fly away.

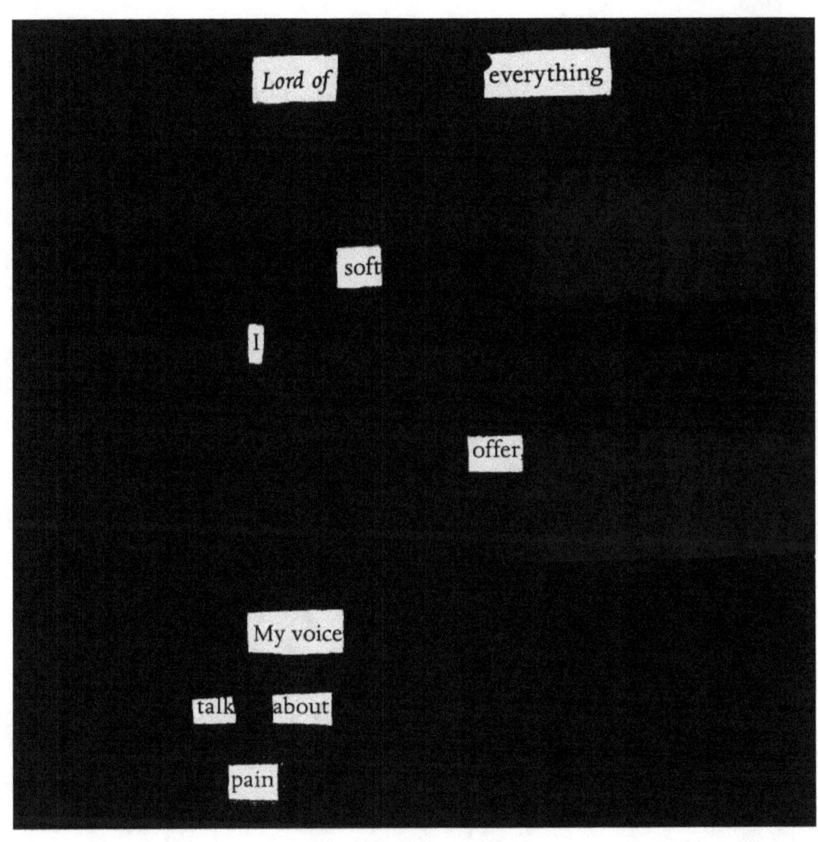

Lord of
everything
soft
I
offer
My voice
talk about
pain

GRAVE

And if,
after my death
the world is still as
cruel as it is,
you both can stand
on my grave
—two pairs of feet,
if only to find a place
to dance and to love,
quietly, without
shame and regret.

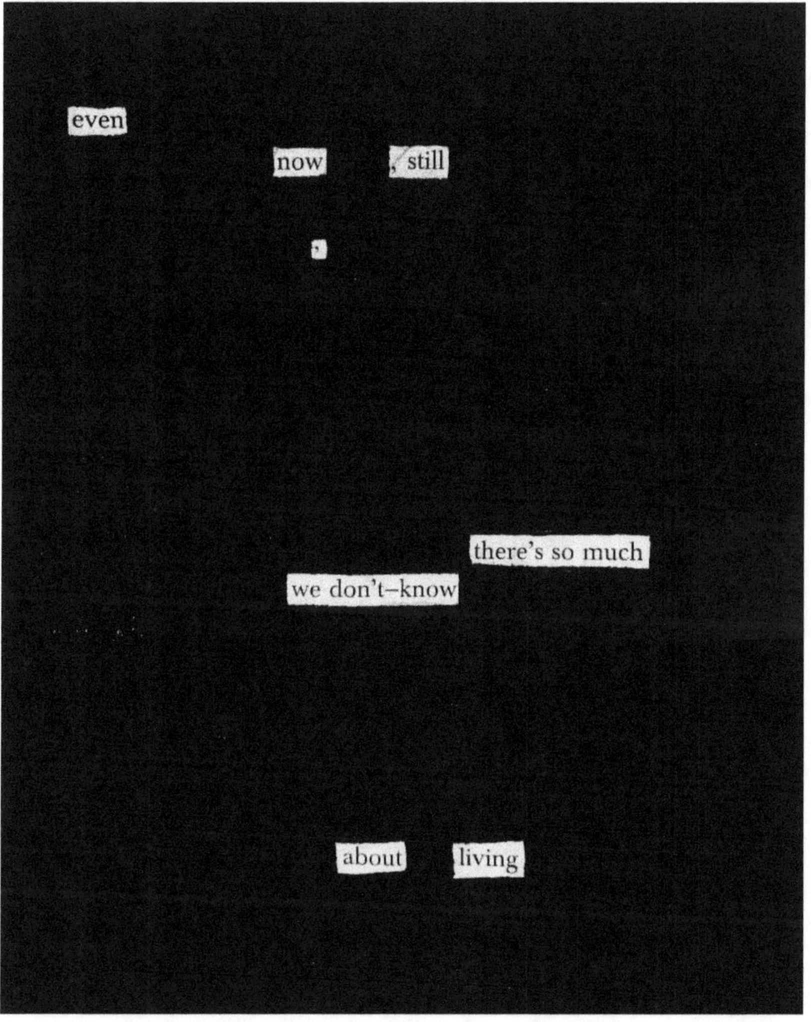
even
now   , still
;
there's so much
we don't–know
about   living

Time will tell
what remains
of us.

CHAOS, AFTER

Maybe one day,
all that's left,
what we owe
each other,

is love.

SUMMER RAIN, VIII

You do not have to fill your sky with clouds;
you do not have to gather them
until they're too heavy to hold your rain.

I do not have to remind you
of the danger that comes
with keeping too much inside.

So pour down as often as you need.
Do not think of it as inconvenience,
do not even apologize.

I would rather get soaked to the skin
just so you can paint your rainbow again.

HOUSE GUESTS

An invitation
only goes so far.
We are made comfortable,
and we wish we could offer
the same.

But there are always rooms
never used,
There are always doors
never opened.

And if there is longing
other than ours,
we never see.

None of us knows.

SUMMER RAIN, IV

Let me be the rain
that washes away
every heartbreak,
every single doubt
about love ever coming back.

Believe – like the earth
that has learned to trust.

I am the rain.
Let me show you
I am not all about
destruction.

Forgiveness? Ah! Yes,
Love said,
that's one of my names.

INTEGRITY VS DESPAIR

Life in a flash
—what have I gained,
what have I given?

One life—
oh, but it is
one.

I hope it was enough,
I hope it made a difference.

love
and never hold back
love

better

on days when it's hard,

STILL A LIFE

Of course, it didn't turn out
the way you wanted to.
Of course, this world broke you.
Of course, you feel betrayed.
Weren't you, before all this,
so in love with life?

Was it one bad mistake?
Was it a chance you let slip away?
Was it a wrong decision, wrong person even?

Who's to say now. The past
has nothing else to offer.
But if you leave it all behind,
if you look ahead,
the future offers itself
to you, saying,

Here is a life
still left to live.
It isn't much to begin
but take it.
Here — make it beautiful.
Do what you can
with what you have.

There's still time.
There's still time.

And   all hope   lived.   that
little thing   grew and grew and lived

LEGACY

oh, to reach for the stars,
to be great,
to pioneer,
to build,
to create,
to inspire—
what valiant pursuits!

but sometimes
to laugh,
to smile,
to make someone smile,
to smell the flowers,
to fall in love
with the most beautiful
little things,

to forgive,
to be gentle,
to be kind,
to be, simply.

might these be
the only things
I will ever do?

very well then.

DOXOLOGY

Less asking,
more thanking—
may I be humbled
each time I pray.

May I learn to see
the good in every day,
and if I can't find it,
may I learn
to be it.

HOPE FOR US

I want you to know
that no matter how cruel
or divided this world
may seem sometimes,

there is hope
for us.

There is a future.
There is a chance
for love.

It only takes
one
indefatigable heart.

But if you have
to believe in
one thing —
believe in LOVE.

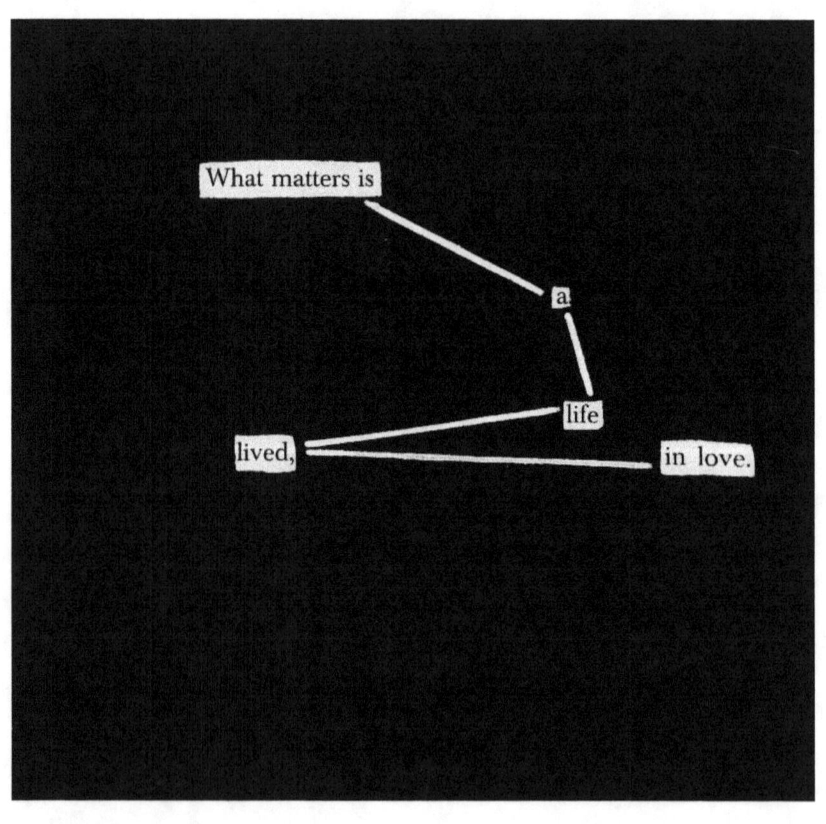
What matters is
a
life
lived,
in love.

I will love,
beyond all
measure,
all over again.

THE DREAMER

So, it has all come to this—
This void, us floating in space.
Dark after dark after dark.
From a distance the stars
are pinpoints of light.

It didn't always feel this way.
There was a time
when anything seemed possible,
like when, many years ago,
a boy in the middle of the night
swung his window open
to find me standing there.

Are... you... The Dreamer?
It was you—the boy, curious eyes,
innocent in your optimism.
I am, I replied, though hesitant.
Very well then, take me there—
you, pointing to the stars,
your finger a glittering magic wand.

And how could I say no?
How could I break a tender heart?
Even now, lying asleep,
that face, same innocent face,
I can't bear to tell you
when you awake and find us
here—this dark place called
Nothing
          —that this is where it ends.

So I took your tiny hand, and on a
long journey we embarked.
First the long Road of Foolish Youth,
past the Cathedral of Could-Have-Been,
Cemetery of Dead Dreams,
The Grand Museum of Regret, and then,

we launched into space, for what
in the beginning seemed an adventure
of a lifetime, a final mission
to make things right before we realized
that perhaps we weren't made for this.
Perhaps, some dreams are not for us.
By then, we were already tired.
Gasping for air, weightless,
we wandered aimlessly in the dark.

You woke up to find me weeping, here now,
million miles above. "I'm sorry."
That was all I could say in between sobs.
But you understood.
And you let me cry for some time.

Don't be silly. You got me so far—
you, wise in your optimism.
What good is it if we'll never get there?
We'll never get there if we stop.
But child, I am so tired.
Very well then, I'll take you there.

And how could I say no?
How could I give up now?
Even now, many years passed and it's still
your same infectious enthusiasm.
You... are... The Dreamer. *We are one.*

So you took my calloused hand, and on
a journey we embarked, past some giant clouds
of dust and gas, remnants of a past, but a beginning
of something bright.
Closer and closer and closer.

We can make it, you know?
Don't you see it?
We are almost there.
Don't you see it?

I see it now. There.
Amidst the burning light of stars I see it—
faint and gentle but unmistakable.

We can make it. We are possible.

IV.

ARENA

This isn't all —
what I know
of you, what
you know of
me.

This isn't all,
but it's enough
for now.

CLIMB INTO LOVE

What if to love
is not to fall
but to climb.

What if to love
is not to sink
into the abyss
but to ascend
into new heights.

What if to love
is to see the world
in a different light
—the same one, only
now more beautiful
than it ever was.

ARRIVAL

And what else brings more
promise than the arrival of love?

You look like the days ahead—
lying here, in bed with me,
the outline of your body a
cavalcade of future memory.

My love, it is too early.

Yes, it is.
I know.
It is dawn, but already
the day is ripe
with possibility.

UNDER THE MOONLIGHT EVERYONE BECOMES A LOVER

I would never wish
for eternal sunshine.
The sun is too proud
to let us admire its light.

But the moon—
I could sit here
for a thousand nights,
you
staring at the fullness
of it,
and me
looking at your eyes,
how they sparkle
in the dark.

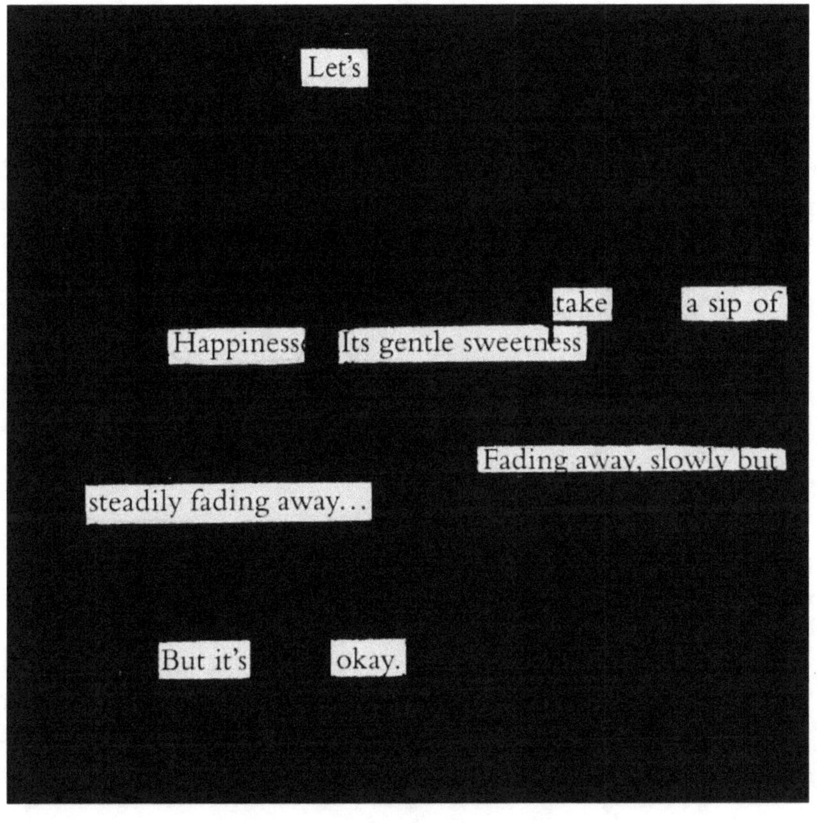

Let's
take
a sip of
Happiness
Its gentle sweetness
Fading away, slowly but
steadily fading away…
But it's
okay.

SAVOUR

COMPLETE COMBUSTION

Be the air that I breathe,
and in time, burn me blue
as I melt with you.

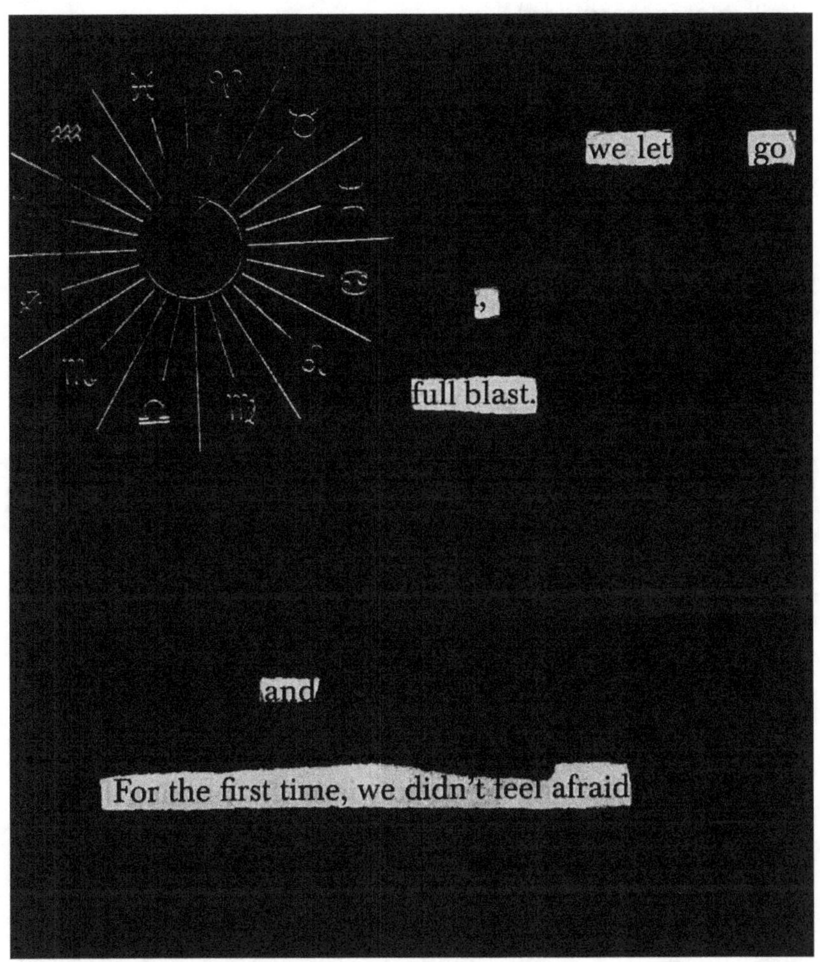
we let   go

,

full blast.

and

For the first time, we didn't feel afraid

ALL THE STARS WE COULDN'T SEE

One of these nights,
all the stars we couldn't see
will shine in the studded sky.

And all our doubts will disappear,
and all will make sense before our eyes.

(There are things we only see
in the darkest of dark.)

We will trace them
into constellation of our own,
and it will be as if our fingers
have always known.

They will call it discovery;
we'll call it home.

in
his eyes
all I see is myself,
And
reflected
it's
so
beautiful

STRIP

I would never have trouble
stripping down in front of you,
if you asked. What is a body
but skin and bones and lust.

But if you really want to see me
naked, in a whole lot less,
to discover all the ugly scars
I have long kept hidden,
if you want me to show you
the most sensitive, most
vulnerable parts of me —

then do not ask for my body;
ask for and make love
with my poetry.

it was a spectacle.
the way they
leaned into each other's shoulders and
looked forward

BECAUSE PERHAPS THE SUN AND THE MOON SHALL ALSO ONE DAY MEET

Until your days are my days
and my nights, your nights,

and the only distance left to conquer
is the space between our shoulders

when I reach for your hand, until then,
send me the sun and I will, the moon

so when the world turns we could
pretend I am waking up to your warmth

and that sliver of light on your face
are my lips kissing you

goodnight

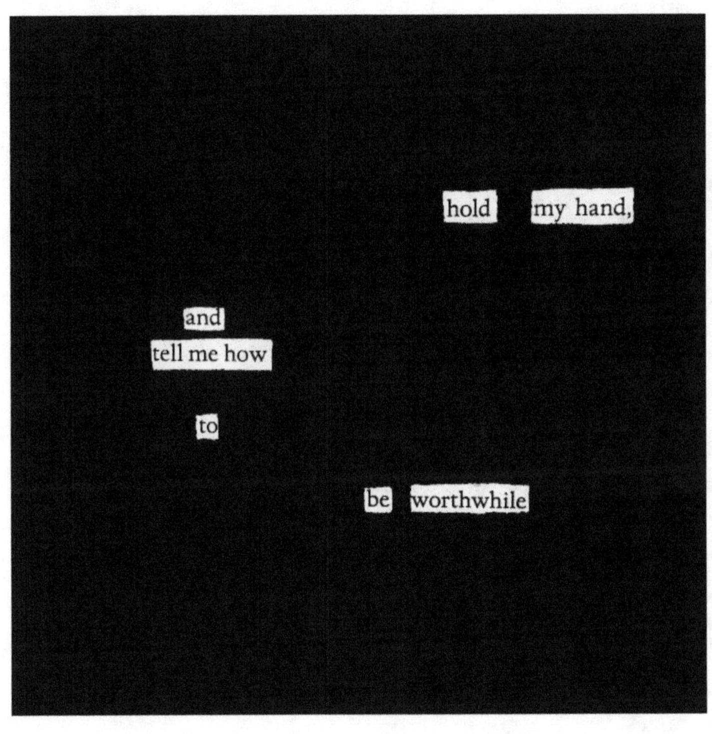

hold   my hand,

and
tell me how

to

be   worthwhile

LIFE WITH YOU

This I say
with the certainty
of night and day:

I wouldn't have it
any other way.

FOR WHAT YOU ARE,
FOR WHAT I AM

What heartbreak,
what pain
can we bring each other
that we haven't already caused
ourselves?

Love is sorrow
just as much as
it is bliss.

Show up at my door
with a lifeful of baggage
for all I care.

Let's unpack it together.

Let
me
want you
, please.

Because even on
nights like this
I will love you,
more and more.
I promise you this.

WILDLY WE LOVE

A piece of untamed wilderness
—something unfamiliar,
undomesticated, ungrounded—
it's what we imagined love to be.

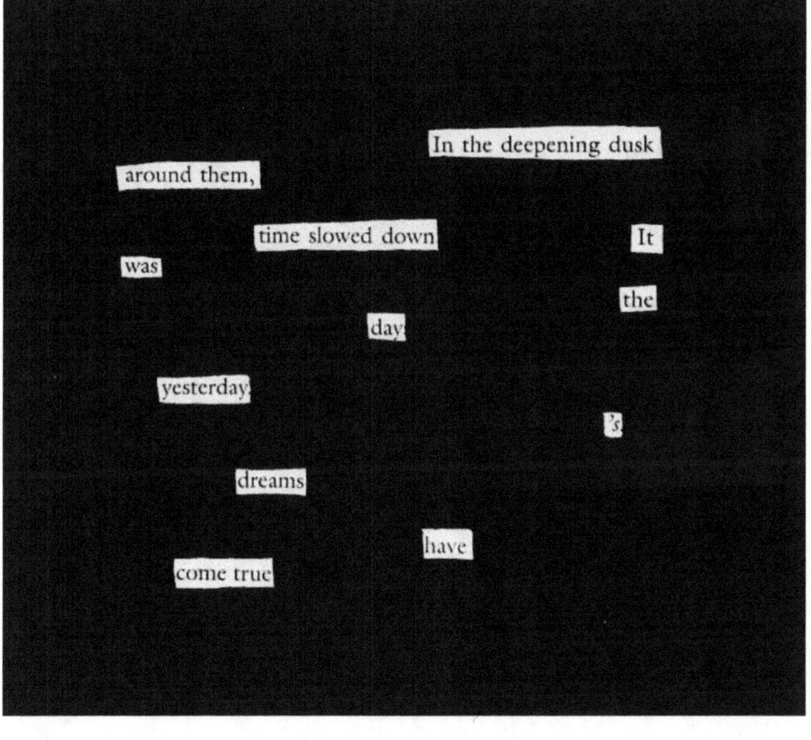

In the deepening dusk
around them,
time slowed down
It
was
the
day
yesterday
's
dreams
have
come true

FOREVER, A SECOND

A kiss—

call it magic,
call it holy,
call it any other name.

It matters not, but how
it made us feel
—that for one surreal second,
it was you and me.
Nothing ever existed,
just this moment.

And my love,
didn't we taste
eternity?

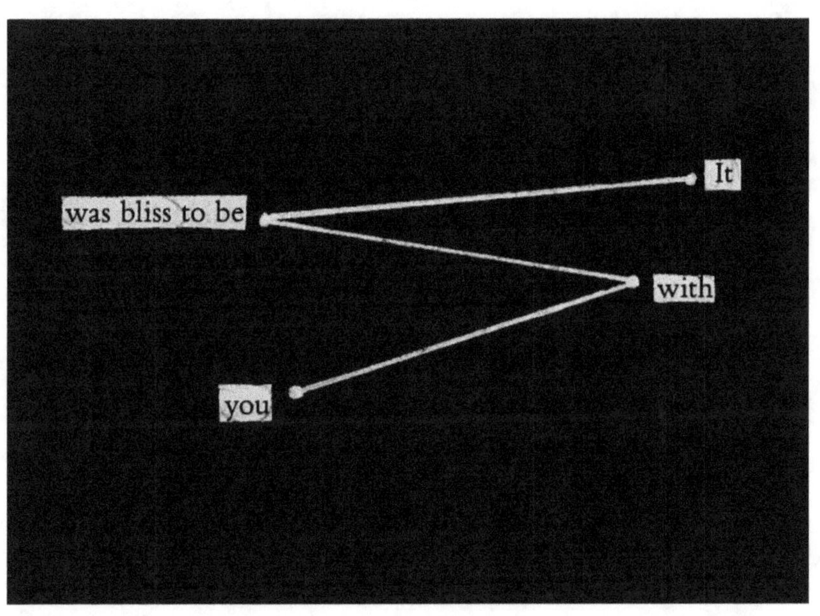
It
was bliss to be
with
you

LOVE IS NOT

a destination;
love is journey, in and of itself.

Love is not a state;
love is action.

One ought not to say
I want to be in love.
Rather, *I want to grow in love.*

For love changes;
love changes us.

For better or for worse,
one who has ever truly loved
shall never be the same again.

CONSTANT

And the snows fell
and melted,
and the flowers bloomed
and withered,
and the trees shed
their leaves.

But the mountain remained,
seasons and seasons hence.
I wake up each day
and it is there, always.

lea   d

me

toward a life

of possibility

what could

happen

is a surprise

, each a tiny snapshot, of

the

fanciful

brilliance of

this   life

HEARTH

At the murmur of flame
their fingers touched.
"Home," they said.

MORNING WALKS

To walk
slower
and match
your pace.

To look at you
and ask
what you need
or want,
or tell you
what I need
or want.

To hold
your hand.

Remind me
of these things.
Remind me
that this time
and onward,

I am not walking
alone anymore.

A REASSURANCE

And when, in times of doubt
you say you are not enough,
I will wear the same smile
I'm sure you'll recognize
from all those times
you made me feel
so loved.

BELIEVER

I look at you
and suddenly
my faith is
unshakeable.

Someone
must have known;
someone put you here.

Suddenly,
I am certain
no other place exists,
none more perfect for me
than this one,
this one
with you in it.

I am meant to be here
—this, the best
of all
possible worlds.

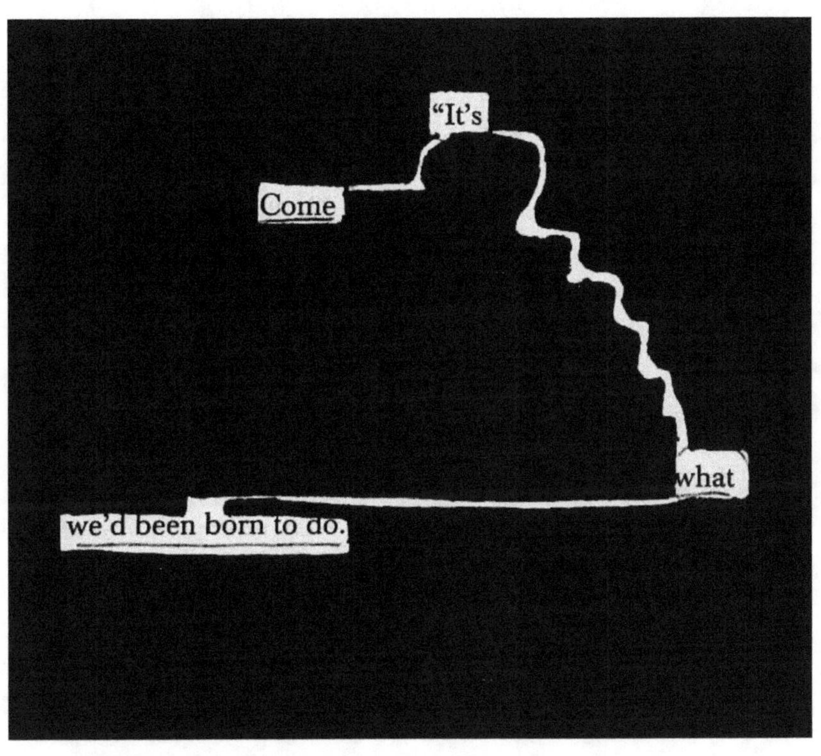

"It's
Come
what
we'd been born to do.

SOMEWHERE, WE NEVER END

Toward the dying light
we will run.
Toward every new horizon
we will set our eyes.

We are now
chasing sunsets,
though our feet
be constantly tired,
though our breaths
be out all the time.

We will trade exhaustion
for grandeur, for that
one golden hour
that will last forever.

And it will be gorgeous.

You and I — one day
we will be nothing more
than a legend.
But at least in the stories
we'd still be running,

wild and free.

acknowledgments

This second book would not have been written if not for the support, big or small, of my family (Nanay, my siblings, the Claritos and the Perezes. Thank you for the gift of family); my friends (there's not a lot of you, but you know you're the real deal); and my readers on social media. I hold deep gratitude for those of you who believe in me.

Thank you, Ryan, for creating the cover art. I know you only agreed because of that weirdly accurate horoscope. Thank you, Caroline, for the cover design. It was a pleasure working with you. Bless all those who create beautiful things.

Majority of this book was written on the land of the Peetabeck Inninuwuk on the Mushkegowuk Traditional Territory. It was completed on the traditional land of the Mississaugas of the Anishinaabe, the Haudenosaunee, and the Wendat. I am incredibly grateful for the land I am hosted on and the generosity of the Indigenous People of Canada.

r.c. perez is a high school teacher and poet from Toronto, Canada. He was born in a rural town in the Philippines, surrounded by rice fields. At the height of the COVID-19 pandemic, he worked on his first book of poetry called *Magic of the Modest*, which was published in 2021. He shares his work on social media under the handle @ignovionwrites.

praise for r.c. perez

"R.C. Perez is a poet who eloquently conveys human emotions' intricacies, leaving readers with a heart swelled with feelings."

—LA Weekly

"Perez offers poems that help us sort the complexities of the human experience, while also leaving us feeling a sense of wonder and hope about what may come."

—Shereads

praise for magic of the modest

"A relaxed sigh in book form…"

—Thomas Chapman on Goodreads

"…raw yet very inspirational, dealing with the problems of everyday life…the poems seek to warm your heart and touch your soul."

—John Kerry on Goodreads

www.ingramcontent.com/pod-product-compliance
Lightning Source LLC
Chambersburg PA
CBHW061732050726
47598CB00002B/457